MONSTER

Duncan Macmillan

MONSTER

OBERON BOOKS
LONDON

First published in 2007 by Oberon Books Ltd
521 Caledonian Road, London N7 9RH
Tel: 020 7607 3637 / Fax: 020 7607 3629
e-mail: info@oberonbooks.com
www.oberonbooks.com

A catalogue record for this book is available from the British Library.

Cover photograph © Jonathan Oakes

ISBN: 1 84002 759 2 / 978-1-84002-759-4

Printed in Great Britain by Antony Rowe Ltd, Chippenham.

For mum

In memory of Emma Bailey
(May 1983–May 2007)

Acknowledgements

Jacob Murray, Jo Combes, Sarah Frankham, Braham Murray, Greg Hersov and everyone else at the Royal Exchange, thank you for your encouragement and support. Bruntwood, and the competition readers, judges and presenters: Chris Smith, Brenda Blethyn, Kwame Kwei-Armah, Nicholas Hytner, Michael Oglesby, Ben Keaton, Kathy Burke, Tom Courtenay, Susannah Harker, Maxine Peake, Pete Postlethwaite, Roy Williams.

Clare Lizzimore, Simon Stephens, Leo Butler, Ola Animashawun, Nina Lyndon, Lucy Dunkerly, Laura McCluskey, Emily McLaughlin, Pippa Ellis, Roxana Silbert, George Perin, Nina Steiger, Max Stafford-Clark, Chris Campbell, Ben Jancovic, Dawn Walton, Rachael Stevens, Steve Waters, Kate Pakenham, Sonja Linden, Sarah Woods, Levi Addai, Lyndsey Turner, Jenny Maddox, Amy Rosenthal, Gugu Mbatha-Raw, Jamie Cullum, Bola Agbaje, Mike Harris, Kate Harris, Mike Bartlett, Nick Gill, Morgan Lloyd Malcolm, Simon Vinnicombe, Rachel Wagstaff, Jessica Cooper, Jessica Sarbo, Effie Woods, my family.

Duncan was supported in writing this play by the Peggy Ramsay Foundation.

'The monster a child knows best and is most concerned with [is] the monster he feels or fears himself to be.'

– BRUNO BETTELHEIM

'You made your children what they are […] These children that come at you with knives, they are your children. You taught them. I didn't teach them. I just tried to help them stand up […] You can project it back at me, but I am only what lives inside each and every one of you. My father is your system […] I am only what you made me. I am a reflection of you.'

– CHARLES MANSON

Characters

TOM

DARRYL

JODI

RITA

A white room. A white table and two white chairs. They remain onstage until the final scene.

Monster won Second Prize in the Bruntwood Playwriting Competition for the Royal Exchange, part of the Manchester International Festival, and was first performed at the Royal Exchange Theatre, Manchester, on 20 June 2007, with the following cast:

TOM, Andrew French

DARRYL, Mikey North

JODI, Sarah-Louise Young

RITA, Mary Jo Randle

Director Jacob Murray

Designer Louis Price

Lighting Richard Owen

Sound Claire Windsor

Voice Mark Langley

1

Morning. School.

The sound of children running, laughing, shouting, screaming.

TOM sits at the table. He looks at his watch and straightens his tie. He sits rigidly upright, staring at the door.

,

He glances at his shoes, then back at the door.

,

He rubs one of his shoes on the back of his trousers, then leans down to look at it.

He sits back up.

,

He leans down and rubs his shoe with his sleeve.

DARRYL enters, his hooded top hanging off one shoulder, underneath which he wears a burgundy school sweatshirt. He is chewing. He drops his bag on the floor and stares at TOM.

TOM sees him and stands.

,

TOM Darryl.

Sit down.
Sit down Darryl.

,

Alright, let's run through some rules.
First, and most important, is that you get here on time for the lesson to begin. That means before the lesson is due to start. That way you'll be ready to go.

Second, the bag goes on the hook.

DARRYL looks at the hook.

,

Sit down please Darryl.

I'm Tom,

> *TOM extends his hand for DARRYL to shake. DARRYL stares at it.*

I'm going to be with you for the rest of this year.

,

> *TOM withdraws his hand.*

,

Third, there's no eating during lessons. What are you eating?

> *DARRYL opens his mouth and sticks out his tongue, on which is a large blue sweet.*

Bin.

Bin.

In the bin please Darryl.

,

> *DARRYL crunches the sweet in his mouth, then chews it slowly and swallows it, without ever taking his eyes off TOM.*
>
> *Silence.*

Sit down please Darryl.

> *Silence.*

We're not getting off to a good start here are we?

Am I going to have to call your mum?

DARRYL   Don't think so.

TOM   I will.

DARRYL   She's dead init?

,

TOM	I'm sorry.
DARRYL	Live with my nan.
TOM	Sorry Darryl.
DARRYL	What you done?
TOM	No, really I'm
DARRYL	you ain't done nothing.
TOM	No.
DARRYL	Did it herself.

,

DARRYL sits opposite TOM, leaving his bag where it is.

,

TOM	Darryl, do you understand why you've been taken out of lessons?
	Darryl?

,

DARRYL	Yes.
TOM	Why?
DARRYL	'Cause Head of Year's a bitch init?
TOM	No.
DARRYL	Beyatch.
TOM	No.
DARRYL	Wants a smack.
TOM	Darryl
DARRYL	Godzilla.
TOM	Now,
DARRYL	she come up in here now I'd box her down. I'd be like, 'hey, Miss, man, eat this bitch' and she'd be like 'noooo'

and I'd like 'booosch!' like that thing that thing have you seen it, that thing that video mobile

TOM   Darryl,

DARRYL   that 'Happy Slappers'.

TOM   Darryl we don't refer to it as that in this school.

DARRYL   It's wicked.

TOM   What do we refer to it as?

DARRYL   Fucking excellent.

TOM   Common assault.

DARRYL   Oh yeah, yeah. Common assault yeah. Video the common assault on your mobile and send it everyone. It's slammin'.

TOM   Darryl, three students have been excluded this year for

DARRYL   there's this one, yeah, where they get this girl in a headlock, yeah, they hold her so she can't move and then 'bout ten a these guys

TOM   I don't want to hear about that Darryl. I'm not impressed by that.

DARRYL   I got Saddam. What's your number? I'll text it you.

TOM   Will you put that away?

DARRYL   You got Bluetooth?

TOM   Put your phone away.

DARRYL   Have you though?

TOM   Sit properly please Darryl.

DARRYL   Bet you got an old dinosaur phone init? Big cream-coloured brick with antennae and shit.

TOM   Sit on your chair properly please.

DARRYL   Like your crepes init?

TOM   My what?

DARRYL   Your shoes.

                 ,

TOM   What about my shoes?

DARRYL   They're shit.
          Sorry, but they is.
          They're wack.
          You gived them an ikkle bit a scrub and t'ing, polish dem
          up an' that. But dey still cheap init? Laces don't match.
          New laces. Old shoes. You had dem for *time*.

TOM   You're very observant Darryl.

DARRYL   True dat. Keep my eyes open init?

TOM   I'm impressed.

DARRYL   Can I axe you a question?

TOM   Darryl,

DARRYL   can I though?

TOM   No. Not right now.

DARRYL   Gosh man. Just want to arks a question init?

                 ,

          TOM sits down.

TOM   What do you want to know?

DARRYL   What would you do, yeah, if you were on a plane and
          someone was like 'you're all gonna die, I'm gonna fly this
          bitch into a wall'?

TOM   Darryl, why don't we look at the

DARRYL   would you be scared?

TOM   Darryl, come on let's

DARRYL   would you though? I bet you would.
          I bet you'd shit yourself.

TOM   Darryl, alright, listen,

DARRYL   did you go to this school?

TOM   No, I

I went to school in Surrey.

DARRYL   Is it?

TOM   Yes.

DARRYL   Why?

DARRYL has taken a lighter from his pocket.

TOM   Because that's where I lived.
Will you sit on your chair properly Darryl?

DARRYL   Well posh init?
Surrey?

TOM   Not really.

DARRYL ignites the lighter.

Darryl give me that. You know the rules.

DARRYL runs a finger through the flame.

DARRYL   Can I axe you a question?

TOM   Give that to me. Now.

DARRYL   Why?

TOM   Because of fire regulations.

DARRYL   I'm not gonna burn the school down.

TOM   Just give it to me please.

,

DARRYL   Alright.

DARRYL pushes the lighter across the table.

TOM reaches over, takes it and puts it in his pocket.

,

TOM   Tell me how you feel your lessons have been going. How about History?

DARRYL   Can I axe you a question?

TOM   If you do some work you can ask all the questions you want.

DARRYL   Can I?

TOM   Absolutely.

DARRYL   Can I axe you one now though?

TOM   Work first.

DARRYL   But it's important.

TOM   Is it?

DARRYL   Yeah. I really think I should be allowed to arks it.

,

TOM   Well, I'm sorry, you'll have to do a little bit of reading for me first. And stop picking your teeth.

DARRYL   But I won't be able to do anything 'til I've axed my question. Believe. Can't concentrate, you get me?

TOM   Where's your History book?

DARRYL   I'm serious.

TOM   So am I.

,

DARRYL   What would happen, yeah, if

TOM   Darryl, I'm not answering any questions until

DARRYL   this is about History.

TOM   Is it?

DARRYL   Yes man, Sir. 'Bout the stuff we've been doing in History bruv.

TOM   Darryl,

DARRYL   it's historical.
His-tor-i-cal.

,

TOM   Go on.

,

DARRYL   What would happen, yeah, if
          I mean, what would you do, yeah

          what if you

TOM   if you don't have a question then

DARRYL   I do man, chillax. I'm phrasing it, yeah?

          Gosh.

          ,

          What if, yeah
          if you, like, woke up one day and both your legs had been
          blown off what would you do?

          'Cause in History this guy was in his house and a bomb
          landed boom! Right on his house, yeah, and he woke up
          and he didn't have any legs.

          ,

TOM   What's your question?

DARRYL   Are you deaf?

TOM   No.

DARRYL   Do you have a hearing problem though?

TOM   Darryl, I just didn't understand your question.

DARRYL   Didn't understand.

TOM   No.

DARRYL   Wasn't clear enough for you is it?

TOM   That's right.

DARRYL   Question was, yeah,
          listen up Surrey.
          What would you do

if you woke up without legs?

,

TOM What would *you* do?

DARRYL I don't know.
It'd be well bad.

TOM Do you know why the war began? How it started?

DARRYL Whose fault?

TOM Yes.

DARRYL Blame game.

TOM If you like.

,

DARRYL What would happen, yeah, if you got both your legs
blowed off and your arms blowed off?

And your head blowed off?
What would you do?

TOM Where's your History book?

,

DARRYL History book.

TOM Where is it Darryl?

,

DARRYL On a shelf.

TOM On a shelf.

DARRYL Shelf in a room.

TOM Darryl, I'm not impressed.

DARRYL It's on a shelf man, in the room.

TOM Darryl

DARRYL in a building

TOM Darryl

DARRYL   let me finish.

TOM   We can do without the book.

DARRYL   Can I axe you a question?

TOM   No.

DARRYL   Are you gay?

TOM   Darryl, that is really none of

DARRYL   are you though?

TOM   That's not relevant.

DARRYL   Do you love cock?

TOM   Darryl,
I

I don't appreciate being asked questions like that.

DARRYL   Is it?

TOM   Yes.

DARRYL   You don't appreciate it?

TOM   It's inappropriate.

DARRYL   Oh right.
Don't appreciate those kind of questions is it?

TOM   That's right.

DARRYL   It's inappropriate.

TOM   Exactly.

,

DARRYL   You are though init?

TOM   No.
I'm not. Actually.

I've got a girlfriend.

DARRYL   Have you?

TOM   Yes.

DARRYL   Have you though?

TOM   Darryl, History.

DARRYL   Because Mr Winters in upper school has got kids and he's a bandit.

TOM   Well, I don't know about Mr Winters.

DARRYL   You saying he is?

TOM   No, I'm saying I don't know him.

DARRYL   I fucking knew it. Bender.

TOM   Darryl, we don't use language like that in this school.

DARRYL   Don't we?

TOM   We don't.

DARRYL   Fucking or bender?

TOM   What?

DARRYL   What words? Fucking or bender? Or fucking bender?

TOM   Where's your History book?

DARRYL   What book?

TOM   The book you've been using in History.

DARRYL   Haven't got a book.

TOM   What have you got?

DARRYL   Ain't got nuffing.

TOM   In your bag.

DARRYL   In my bag.

TOM   What have you got in your bag?

DARRYL   Ain't you listening?

TOM   Your bag's empty?

DARRYL   What did I just say?

TOM   Why do you have an empty bag?

DARRYL   Is she fit?

TOM   What? Who?

DARRYL   Your bitch. She blonde?

TOM   Darryl, that's none of your business, and please don't

DARRYL   that's you init? Down with the swirl.

TOM   Darryl,

DARRYL   she a screamer?

TOM   Darryl, why do you think you're not in lessons?

,

DARRYL   'Cause I bit Kieran.

TOM   No. Did you?

DARRYL   Bit his head.

TOM   Why?

DARRYL   Oh, you know.

TOM   No, I don't.

DARRYL   Yeah you do, you know sometimes it's like
you know sometimes you kind of like

just don't
fit.
Like you're a

no matter what you do nobody really gets you. You get
me?

TOM   Yes.

DARRYL   Which shouldn't matter because they're all they're all just
cunts anyway. They're all fucking

just want to fucking

DARRYL kicks the table.

,

does my head in.

TOM   Okay.

DARRYL   It's like at Mum's funeral, yeah, bunch a people in this
           church all hushed up. No sound, everyone just sat there
           and I wanted to shout something, you get me?

                ,

TOM   Yes. Yes I do.

DARRYL   Just holler. Just shout some fucking, sorry, some bad words
           or some shit. Or just scream loud as I could. Or, like,
           when school took us to the museum and I just wanted to
           break everything.
           I didn't. Didn't touch nothing. Kept hands in pockets.
           It's like with Nan's special glasses, you know

                DARRYL holds his hand up as if holding a glass.

           like crystal or whatever, her posh stuff I just want to drop
           it. Or her angels. The house is full of fucking statues of
           bitches with wings and fat flying naked kids. Sometimes
           I go a bit Mariah Carey and dash one at a wall. A bit
           Barrymore. You know fire extinguishers?

TOM   Do I know

DARRYL   I just want to let them off. I done it once with Kieran, we
           nicked one from his dad's garage and let it off round the
           back a Safeway's.
           Hyphy.

TOM   What else?

DARRYL   Uh?

TOM   What else do you
           how else do you feel sometimes?

                ,

DARRYL   You know the station?

TOM   Yes.

DARRYL   Sometimes when the train's coming and I'm stood behind someone on the platform and they're well near the edge there's a second when I think I'm gonna ram 'em. Shove 'em square into the train yeah?

TOM   Right.

DARRYL   Don't you get that? Ever?
          Like when you walk past a pregnant woman don't you just want to fucking thump them in the stomach?

TOM   No.

DARRYL   I never done it.

TOM   Darryl, that's really

DARRYL   and like sometimes when I'm helping Nan in the kitchen and her back is turned, she's got this knife in her kitchen, yeah, this fuck off great big fuck and I'll have it in my hand 'cause I'm opening a packet or whatever and she'll be at the sink and she's just a just a just a

TOM   Darryl,

DARRYL   just a cardigan, like a little wall of wool and I'm like

TOM   Darryl, have you ever talked to a

DARRYL   it's intense man, like I got
          not like I've
          not that I'd

TOM   because I really think you should

DARRYL   just get vexed though init? Nan says I ain't got no feelings. But it ain't even like that though.

          You know
          sometimes it gets bad yeah and

          I remember what it was like before I was born.
          I remember how it felt.

          You know what Mr

TOM   what?

DARRYL   Your name. Mr

                    ,

TOM   just call me Tom.

DARRYL   Ain't you a real teacher?

TOM   I
            yes. Yes I am.

DARRYL   You ain't though is you? You're from an agency.

TOM   No.

DARRYL   Can't believe dis. Now dey be leavin' me with an agency.
            Well you can go fuck yourself agency. I ain't doin' shit.

TOM   I'm getting back into teaching. I trained in

DARRYL   to rass.

TOM   You're my
            the school is understaffed and
            they've brought me in to

DARRYL   rah rah rah.

TOM   You're kind of like my project.

DARRYL   Oh shit.

TOM   Darryl. Language.

DARRYL   To raatid. Fucking shit.

TOM   Darryl.

DARRYL   You know how many teachers I've had this year?

TOM   How many?

DARRYL   I been out of lessons four months and I've had nine
            support teachers.
            I counted.

TOM   Well, I'm sorry about that.

DARRYL   Bad init?

TOM   It is.

DARRYL   It's shit. It's fucking shit agency.

TOM   Darryl, listen, I'm here at least until the end of the year. I'm not going anywhere.
I've got to be here.

DARRYL   Good for you.

TOM   I mean it.

DARRYL   For your project.

TOM   That's right.

DARRYL looks out of the window.

,

Tell me about what you've been doing in History.

DARRYL   History?

TOM   Yeah.

,

Or Geography?

English?

,

Maths?

DARRYL   Can I axe you a question?

,

TOM   Go on.

DARRYL   Did you always want to be a teacher?

TOM   Why do you ask?

DARRYL   Did you though?

TOM   What do you want to be when you grow up?

I mean, when you leave school.
What do you want to do? Eventually?

DARRYL   Because you're a bit old to be a trainee teacher.

TOM   Not really.

DARRYL   You are though init?

TOM   Not really. And I'm not exactly a

DARRYL   I'm going to be famous.

,

TOM   As what?

DARRYL   Uh?

TOM   Famous as what? Famous for doing what?
You can't just be famous.

DARRYL   Can.

TOM   Alright. But you wouldn't want that.

DARRYL   I would actually.

TOM   It's not a
it's not a brilliant thing to be. Everyone knowing who you
are. You not knowing who they are.

DARRYL   Oh. My. Gosh.

TOM   What?

DARRYL   You're a trainee teacher.

TOM   Yes.

DARRYL   So shut up.

,

TOM   I was
and this is really none of your business, but
I used to have another job and
I decided to retrain as a teacher.

The other job was

it became

,

so, you're right. I am a bit older than most trainee teachers.

Darryl.
Will you sit properly on your

DARRYL   drawn the short straw.

TOM   How do you mean?

DARRYL   This school.

                ,

TOM   I

DARRYL   you heard of Charles Manson?

                ,

TOM   Yes.

DARRYL   He's well famous.

TOM   How did you hear about Manson?

DARRYL   Was you fired?

TOM   When? What?

DARRYL   What job was it?

TOM   It
       I worked in the city.

DARRYL   Oh right. In the city.

TOM   Yes. How did you hear about

DARRYL   big business.

TOM   Yes,
       I suppose so.

DARRYL   Bet you're well loaded.

TOM   I wasn't very high up.

DARRYL   Not high up.

TOM   Middle management.

DARRYL   In the middle yeah?

TOM   Brand management.

DARRYL   Labels.

TOM   Food, not clothing. But, yeah, that's right. Marketing
          certain foods to children. I was

          originally I trained as a
          in psychology. Educational psychology. And I
          I intended to be
          to go into
          education. But in the
          I mean, as it turns out I went into

          business.

          There's a term in psychology known as the educable
          moment when a child is at their most receptive and that's
          something that advertisers are very interested in and

                  '

          Darryl, how did you hear about Charles Manson?

DARRYL   Carl got this DVD yeah, from America. It's wicked.

TOM   Who's Carl?

DARRYL   Nan's boyfriend.

TOM   I'm not sure he should be showing you films like that.

DARRYL   You know what he did?

TOM   Carl?

DARRYL   Manson.

TOM   Yes.

DARRYL   Wicked init?

TOM   No.

DARRYL   Yes it is. It's well good. Painted the walls with blood.
          He's still alive init?

TOM   I don't know.

DARRYL   He is.
          So was you fired then?

TOM   No. No I

DARRYL   you was though, init?

TOM   I wasn't fired.

DARRYL   I bet you was though.

TOM   Who else do you admire?

DARRYL   Ad-what?

TOM   Who else is wicked?

DARRYL   Tupac.

TOM   Why?

DARRYL   He's made like a billion albums since being gunned down.

          DARRYL drums loudly on the table, making the sound of a machine gun.

          Plus UK hip hop is dry.

TOM   Do you talk like this to everyone?

DARRYL   Like what?

TOM   The way you speak. Do you speak that way with everybody or are you just trying to impress me?
          You think you'll impress me by talking that way? Because I'm black.

DARRYL   Shame. Are you being racist?

TOM   I'm just asking you whether you would talk like this to me if I was white like you. If you think that by talking like that we'll have some kind of connection because you think that's how black people talk.

DARRYL   Are you cussing me? You calling me a wangsta?

TOM   A what?

DARRYL   A wigga?

TOM   I'm just asking whether

DARRYL   you ain't black.

,

TOM   Excuse me?

DARRYL   You're from Surrey.

,

TOM   I'm not going to explain or justify my heritage to you Darryl.

DARRYL   You ain't black.

,

TOM looks down at his hands.

,

He takes a deep breath and looks back up at DARRYL.

,

TOM   Who else do you admire?

,

DARRYL   Jack the Ripper.

TOM   Okay.

DARRYL   You seen the movie?

TOM   No.

DARRYL   It's well bad.

TOM   Who else?

DARRYL   It's shit.

TOM   Did Carl show that to you?

DARRYL   Was it hard? Your middle job?

,

TOM   It had

    ,

certain pressures.
Certain pressures which made it

it's not what I intended to use my training for and

    ,

I found it difficult to progress.

I was there for a number of years and I was never

or they'd give me jobs that I wasn't really right for and I wasn't quite equipped to

DARRYL   did you meet any celebrities?

TOM   One or two.

DARRYL   Who?

TOM   Darryl, I think you've had enough questions for now.

DARRYL   Who though?

TOM   Darryl, let's do some work.

DARRYL   Oh my gosh. Who?

TOM   Well

DARRYL   Osama Bin Laden.
He's excellent.

TOM   No Darryl, he isn't.

DARRYL   What do you think it would be like to kill someone?

    ,

TOM   I think it would be pretty horrible.

DARRYL   Why?

TOM   It's just about the worst thing you can do.

DARRYL   Why?
What would happen if I did? What would happen to me?

,

TOM   Well,
you'd be put in prison.

DARRYL   Is it?

TOM   For the rest of your life.

DARRYL   How would you do it?

TOM   I wouldn't.

DARRYL   Gun.
Blat blat.

TOM   Darryl, you're wasting time now. Let's

DARRYL   AK47. When you absolutely

TOM   Darryl,

DARRYL   positively

TOM   please Darryl,

DARRYL   have to kill every motherfucker in the room

accept no substitute.

TOM   Very good. Now let's

DARRYL   or just stab them. Like Manson.

DARRYL bangs the table.

Rip 'em apart. That's what I'd do. Get close.
There's this knife in my Nan's kitchen which is

TOM   Darryl.

DARRYL   It ain't even about how though, it's about

TOM   Darryl.

DARRYL   What? You're disrupting my flow man. Cha!

TOM   Do you want me to call senior staff?

DARRYL   Why?

TOM   Because you're not working.

DARRYL   I haven't done anything.

TOM   You're not working.

DARRYL   Yeah, but I ain't done nothing wrong.

TOM   Sit on your chair properly.

DARRYL   You getting pissed off?

TOM   No.

DARRYL   Getting well angry.

TOM   I don't get angry.

DARRYL   Is it?

TOM   Let's just

DARRYL   not ever?

TOM   I'm not like that.

DARRYL   Like what?

TOM   Let's look at History. Alright?

DARRYL   History's *long*.

TOM   History's probably the most important subject.

DARRYL   Why?

TOM   Because

well, because

DARRYL   you don't know, do you?

TOM   Yes.

DARRYL   Do you though?

TOM   Yes.

DARRYL   Except you don't though.

TOM   It's important to know.

DARRYL   Why?

TOM   Well,

History's important to learn about so you don't end up repeating old mistakes.

DARRYL   Might make mistakes is it?

TOM   Exactly.

DARRYL   If I don't learn History?

TOM   That's right.

DARRYL   Like what?

   ,

TOM   Well, like

like all the things that have gone wrong in the world. If we forget about all that, we'll inevitably end up

DARRYL   like wars and shit.

TOM   That's right. Exactly.

DARRYL   Except there's still wars init?

TOM   What, now? Now there's lots, yes.

DARRYL   England's at war init?

TOM   Well, the British government has engaged in

DARRYL   ain't they done their History though? Don't the government know their History?

TOM   What do you know about the world wars?

DARRYL   You seen 'Pearl Harbour'?

TOM   No.

DARRYL   You seen 'Platoon'?

TOM   Darryl, do you know when the First World War began? Will you sit properly on your chair? I'm not telling you again.

   ,

Listen,

if you do well today I'll

I'll give you a sticker.

,

DARRYL   Yeah?

TOM   Yes.

,

DARRYL   Your job, yeah,

TOM   you can only have a sticker if you concentrate for the rest of the lesson.

,

DARRYL   Can I pick which one?

TOM   Which what?

DARRYL   Sticker.

TOM   You haven't earned it yet.

DARRYL   But can I though?

TOM   Yes.
If you work for the rest of the lesson you can choose what sticker you want.

DARRYL   Gold one?

TOM   If you want.

DARRYL   Gold ones are best init?
Blinga blinga.

TOM   Gold ones are the best. Definitely.
But you'll have to work really hard to earn a gold one.

Silence.

DARRYL   What do you want me to do?

2

Evening. House.

TOM has taken his jacket and tie off. JODI sits on the table behind him, massaging his shoulders. She has a tea towel over her shoulder and a glass of wine by her side.

,

TOM   God help me if he ever gets bored of stickers.
Then I really am screwed.

,

She kisses the top of his head.

It's almost enough to make me want to move back to the city.

JODI climbs down from the table. She drains her wine glass.

It's a joke.

JODI   It's not funny.

JODI exits to the kitchen.

TOM   I didn't mean

I'm

,

TOM stares at his shoes.

JODI enters, carrying cutlery and two tall glasses which she places on the table. TOM takes one and stares at it as JODI arranges the cutlery.

JODI   I hope you're hungry.

It's all come out of a book, so it should be good.

,

It's in the oven.
Duck.

Something a bit posh.

TOM is holding the glass in the air as if about to drop it.

,

Tom?

,

I've finished the red.
There's some champagne in the fridge.

Actually Tom, will you do me a favour and fetch it?

JODI is watching him.

,

Tom?

,

TOM   Sorry.
Yes.
Yes I'll go.

Did you say champagne?

JODI   What's wrong?

TOM   I'm sorry.

JODI   What's happening?

TOM   Nothing, I'm fine.
Just tired. It's really starting to

been a long week.

JODI   Have a lie down, I can keep dinner going.

TOM   No, I'm

JODI   do you want a glass of water? I can

TOM   stop being so jumpy.

JODI   I'm not. I'm looking after you.

TOM   I don't need to be

I'm fine.
I'm fine.

,

JODI   Are you hungry?

TOM   Yes.
        Yes I think so.

JODI   Have a drink.

TOM   Alright.

JODI   It's in the kitchen.

,

TOM   Right.

> *TOM stands and puts the glass on the table. He walks to the
> kitchen.*

JODI   Tom.
        Look at me.

> *He does.*

Hey.

,

Hey.

,

He's just a kid.

I love you.
Okay?

,

TOM   Okay.

JODI   Okay?

,

TOM   Yes.

,

He leaves. JODI watches him go, anxiously.

,

She hurriedly takes a candle and some matches from a drawer in the table, and lights it. She takes a small jewellery box from her pocket, opens it and looks at the ring inside. She is very nervous.

She closes the box and places it in front of where he was sitting.

She dims the lights.

She sits at the table.

She checks her appearance, touching her hair and straightening her clothes.

She sits staring at the box, biting her lip.

,

She impulsively grabs the box and hides it.

She blows out the candle and puts her head in her hands.

,

She composes herself.

,

She checks her appearance, touching her hair and straightening her clothes.

She relights the candle.

,

She slowly places the box back where it was.

She checks herself and notices the tea towel, pulls it off her shoulder and sits on it.

TOM enters with the bottle. He is oblivious to the change in lighting.

I couldn't find the glasses.

JODI They're right here.

TOM Oh.

> *TOM smiles.*
>
> *He sits and begins to unwrap the foil from the champagne.*
>
> *JODI watches him nervously.*

,

Thing about Darryl is that I think he could've been quite bright, or at least, not as disruptive, if he'd been brought up better.

JODI Darryl.

TOM That's his name.
I've told you that.

This pasty little white kid who talks like he's straight outta Compton.

> *JODI smiles.*

JODI I still don't get it. I thought the point was you were going to be paired up with a black kid. Be a role model.

TOM Yeah well.
You know, on my first day he even said that I wasn't black.

,

JODI Well,

,

TOM what?

JODI Nothing.

TOM Go on.

JODI No nothing.

Just,

you're not really are you?

TOM   Yes Jodi, I am.

JODI   Yes I know, of course you are.

But you're from Surrey.

TOM   That's what he said, what does that mean? What
difference does that

JODI   just
you're not very
street.

Are you though?

TOM   What does that matter? That's got nothing to do with

JODI   all I mean is that
how many black kids did you know growing up?

TOM   That's completely

JODI   alright. Alright, forget it.

*TOM shakes his head. JODI watches him removing the foil
from the bottle.*

Silence.

And is it? Too late for him?

TOM   What?

JODI   You said he could have been
that he could have, had it not been for

TOM   his parents splitting up, or
you know, his Nan's
partner, he lets him watch all these films.

His mother's dead. She

*TOM stops opening the champagne. He looks up at JODI very
briefly.*

I don't know about his father. Whether he was ever even

JODI   a lot of kids come from broken homes.

TOM   I know.

JODI   A lot of good kids.

TOM   Of course they do, that's not
        I'm not saying

JODI   a lot of kids watch nasty films.

TOM   Yes, I know but

JODI   I did.

TOM   I know that.
        No. I know.

        You're right.

        ,

> *JODI reaches across the table. TOM puts down the bottle and*
> *takes her hands in his.*

JODI   Tom,

TOM   but I do think that he could have been alright with better
        parents. That's all I'm saying.

JODI   I wanted to

TOM   he's got an amazing eye for detail. He continually

        he keeps saying things that amaze me.
        Most of the time he's just
        aggravating
        but sometimes he has these flashes of

JODI   has he been seen by a specialist?

        ,

TOM   What do you mean?

JODI   You know a
        a professional

> *TOM looks away from JODI.*

JODI takes her hands away from TOM.

is he statemented?

TOM   Yes.

JODI   Has someone done an evaluation? You know, a psychological

TOM   I'm sure someone must've

JODI   should he even be in a proper school?

,

TOM   Do you think that's what it is, that he's
he's got something

JODI   I don't know.

Maybe.

,

TOM   No.

No, he's alright.

He's alright. Just disruptive. I'm sure if he grows up a bit and cuts back on the sugar he'll

although
you know,

he mutters.

He mumbles away to himself under his breath. He doesn't think I can hear him.

,

I'm sorry.
Sorry. Gosh, look at me.

JODI   'Gosh'?

TOM   Look at me, have I been this distracted since I started teaching?

JODI   Who says 'gosh'?

TOM   I'm sorry if I've been out of it. It really takes it out of you. Sitting there, one-to-one, it's really

let's have an evening.

    TOM picks up the bottle.

JODI   I'm worried about you.

TOM   I'm fine.

JODI   It's not been long.

TOM   Alright.

JODI   It's only been

TOM   look,
let's not do this alright?

    He puts the bottle back on the table.

JODI   But I
alright, I'm sorry, but I just wanted to say that
just for the record, you made me a promise when we left the city that

TOM   alright.

JODI   Just let me say this.
Please.

    ,

You made me a promise and we made lots of changes.

TOM   I know.

JODI   I made changes.

TOM   I know that.

JODI   You seem to be
you seem to be letting it get to you.

You're supposed to be taking it easy.

    ,

There. I've said it.

TOM   Fine.

JODI   I know everything's probably

TOM   it's fine. It's okay.

        You've said
        you've said what you needed to say and

        you're right.

        Okay?

              ,

JODI   Okay.

        Good.

              ,

        Thanks for letting me just

TOM   is the food alright?

              ,

        JODI looks towards the kitchen.

              ,

JODI   We can leave it a minute.

        Tom,

TOM   I know you're looking out for me and I know

        I know you're worried about me. But I'm fine now.
        Really.

        I'm sorry if I've been boring you with it all.

JODI   Not boring,

TOM   like I don't get enough of this kid at work.

JODI   Tom, I've got something

TOM   I've been really selfish.

JODI   There's something else I need to

TOM   what did you say it was? Duck?

,

JODI   Yeah.

I'll go check on it.

She gets up.

TOM   Do you want a hand?

JODI   I'm alright.

JODI moves towards the kitchen.

TOM notices the jewellery box. He looks up at JODI.

TOM   Jodi?

JODI stops and turns to face him.

JODI   Yeah?

,

TOM   What's this?

She takes a deep breath.

Silence.

TOM picks up the box carefully and opens it.

JODI shifts on the spot, looking towards the kitchen, playing anxiously with her hands.

TOM stares into the box.

,

This is

I mean

is this

,

what is this?

I mean

is it

,

JODI   it is.

,

TOM   Oh.

Wow.

,

Jodi,
we said

I mean,
this is great, it is, it's fantastic, just

we said that we'd only ever get married if
well, not ever, only ever, but
the main reason we'd want to get married is if we
if you

if you were

JODI   I am.

,

TOM   Since when?

,

JODI   Month.

Month and a half.

Nearly two months.

,

TOM   Oh.

Silence.

JODI   I haven't been able to tell you.

,

Sorry.

TOM   No, no don't

JODI I just wanted to

TOM   it's great, it's all

JODI shit.

TOM   No, it's

JODI shit.

> *TOM stands.*

TOM   Oh, listen, no don't

JODI I thought you'd be
      I thought it's what you wanted, that it would

TOM   just give me a second.

> *JODI is trying not to cry.*

JODI I'm so scared. I'm so scared Tom.

TOM   I

      I'm

> *Silence.*

> *TOM looks at the ring.*

> '

> *He takes it out of the box.*

> *Silence.*

this is beautiful.

> '

Yes of course I'll marry you.
Of course I will.
I love you.

JODI Are you sure?

TOM   Yes.

Yes yes yes.

,

Thank you.

,

JODI nods.

,

JODI The
I'll just check on the

TOM leave it a second.

JODI It'll dry out, I have to

TOM Jodi

JODI see if it's

JODI exits.

,

TOM looks at the ring.

,

He sits down at the table.

3

Morning. School.

TOM sits at the table, rubbing his ring finger.

,

DARRYL enters, his hooded top hanging off his shoulder.

DARRYL Wha gwan?

He drops his bag on the floor and paces around the room, looking at the walls.

TOM Sit down please Darryl.

DARRYL What's up wit dis place today?

TOM Nothing. Everything's

DARRYL dem's all wearing suits init? All the teachers got new do's.

TOM New

DARRYL haircuts.

You ain't.

TOM No.

DARRYL starts jogging on the spot.

DARRYL You got the same gear on as always init agency?
Worn the same shit for months.

TOM Sit down please.

DARRYL All been spruced up everywhere. Posh glasses in the canteen. Tablecloths.

I weren't supposed to be in there.

TOM No, you were supposed to be here ten minutes

DARRYL just wanted to try that thing that thing, you know that thing that pulling the tablecloth and letting the glasses all smash.

TOM   Actually Darryl, I think the point is to keep the glasses
           intact.

           ,

           You didn't, did you?

DARRYL   Nah man. Dey wouldn't let me near.

TOM   Now, Darryl, I've put together a list of attainable targets
           for

DARRYL   inspections init?

TOM   Not exactly.

DARRYL   Last time there was inspections I went out in the minibus.
           Five days, five field trips.

           DARRYL starts throwing punches into the air.

TOM   It's not exactly

DARRYL   all us trouble-makers. Ruffnicks. Stuffed in a minibus and
           shipped out of school.

           Sent the shit teachers out with us and all.

           Guess that be you now agency.

           Bowling, ice-skating.

TOM   Yes, well, it's not exactly

DARRYL   farm, glass-blowing. Fucking glass-blowing.

TOM   The school is having a visitation from

DARRYL   inspectors init?

TOM   No, it's

           it's someone from the government.
           They wanted to look around a school which

           DARRYL stops jogging.

DARRYL   is it Tony Blair?

TOM   No Darryl.

DARRYL   It is though init?

TOM   I'm sure the Prime Minister has more important things to
          do than

DARRYL   oh my gosh.

TOM   Sssh.

DARRYL   Don't sssh me.

TOM   Just keep it down alright?

DARRYL   Is he coming in here?

TOM   No. There's

          as far as I understand, there's going to be a formal tour
          around the sports grounds and the new science block and
          then a gathering in the canteen.

DARRYL   A gathering.

TOM   That's right.

DARRYL   What dey looking for?

TOM   They want to see how the school is doing. What it's like.

DARRYL   'Cept they won't though.

TOM   Well, they're here.

DARRYL   Yeah, but this ain't the school. Have you been out there?
          Everyone movin' bookie, looking dodge. It's like that film,
          have you seen it?

TOM   No.

DARRYL   That 'Dawn of the Dead'. 'Stepford Wives' or some shit.

TOM   Well, anyway, we need to keep
          our voices
          down.

DARRYL   Is it?

          Silence. They look at each other.

          DARRYL starts jogging on the spot.

Can I go on the computers later?

TOM   We'll have to do some work first.

DARRYL   But you said.

TOM   You're not going on without doing some good work.

DARRYL   Can't I go on now?

TOM   Nope.

DARRYL   Beg you do.

TOM   No Darryl.

DARRYL   Why?

TOM   Because

because it's a privilege not a

DARRYL   you don't know do you?

TOM   I'm trying to tell you.

DARRYL   'Cept you don't though.

DARRYL throws some punches into the air.

TOM   Sit down Darryl.

DARRYL   How about if I sit down at the computers?

TOM   No.

DARRYL   Why?

TOM   Because

alright, listen

how about we do ten minutes concerted work now

DARRYL   on the computers.

TOM   Let me finish. Ten minutes of excellent work now and then I'll set you a project for the rest of the lesson for which you can use the Internet.

DARRYL stops boxing.

DARRYL   Project.

TOM   A project.

DARRYL   PJs.

TOM   Hmm?

DARRYL   From the PJs init?
          Projects?
          NYC.
          East Coast hip hop.
          You get me?

                  ,

TOM   I've no idea what you just said.

          DARRYL starts boxing again.

DARRYL   Do I get a sticker?

TOM   If you complete the project.

DARRYL   Gold one?

TOM   Absolutely.

DARRYL   Will you write down that I did good in my homework
          book?

TOM   Yes.

DARRYL   Will you tell Godzilla?

TOM   Darryl,

DARRYL   Head a Year. The beast.

TOM   I'll tell the Head of Year that you did well.

DARRYL   Can I go back into class?

TOM   I'll talk to her Darryl, but I really don't think that

DARRYL   why?

TOM   Darryl, you know why.

DARRYL   Shit agency, I mean Sir, man, Kieran don't even care anymore. Believe.
We're mates init? Bredren.
I never even bit him that hard. Barely left a mark, you get me?

TOM   Darryl, that's not the point.

DARRYL   Arks him brah. Axe Kieran if he's bothered.

TOM   Darryl,

DARRYL   call 'im.

TOM   Put your phone away Darryl.

DARRYL   Just give 'im a ring init. Ringadingazinga.

TOM yawns.

Am I boring you?

TOM   No, I just

DARRYL   keeping you up agency?

TOM   I just haven't had as much sleep lately as I'd

,

sorry.

DARRYL   Whatever.

TOM   Darryl, will you sit down please?

DARRYL   I'm pacing. Let a man walk.

TOM   What have you had at break? Did you have a fizzy drink? Sweets?
I thought we'd decided that you shouldn't

DARRYL   was thirsty bruv. Nothing quenches a thirst quite like the real t'ing.

TOM   Darryl, don't you remember we had a conversation about

DARRYL   yeah yeah yeah, healthy greens and fruits.

TOM   And you told your nan?

DARRYL   I tell her. Woman cooks a mean meat and rice.

TOM   Darryl sit down.

DARRYL   What harm am I doing?

TOM   Darryl,

DARRYL   what harm though?

TOM   Darryl,

DARRYL   what harm though?

TOM   Sit.
          Now.

          DARRYL stops pacing. He stands staring at TOM.

          ,

          I am *not* in the mood today Darryl. Okay?

          ,

          Sit down.

          ,

          I'm going to count to ten.

          One.
          Two.
          Three.

DARRYL   Gosh man why are you so dry?

TOM   Four.

DARRYL   Why you act like you got stick up your rass?

TOM   Five.

DARRYL   Is it 'cause you had a breakdown at your old job?

          Sat in your garage with the engine running.

          ,

TOM   Six.

DARRYL   It is though init? You went a bit

>   *DARRYL whistles and twirls his finger round his ear.*

TOM   seven.

DARRYL   Girl in upper school's cousin used to work with someone who knew you and she said something about why you can't be a proper teacher just agency or whatever 'cause you went fruit-loops.

>   Says you thumped your girl.

>   Had a breakdown at work. Went schizo and your bird made you jack it in.

>   That's what I reckon.

TOM   Sit down.

DARRYL   Insane in the membrane.

TOM   Sit.

DARRYL   Don't you know I'm loco?

TOM   Stop it.

DARRYL   Or what? You gonna smack me down?

TOM   I'm warning you.

DARRYL   Why'd you do that for? Why did you hit your girl for?

TOM   Shut up.

>   *DARRYL throws punches into the air, staring at TOM.*

DARRYL   Nobody's supposed to know that is they? About you going Bobby Brown?
>   Wouldn't a got the job otherwise.

TOM   Shut up.

>   *DARRYL moves closer to TOM.*

DARRYL   Or what? You going to give me a smack? Gonna lick me in head? I'd love to see that.

>   *TOM stands.*

TOM   Shut up.

DARRYL   You best raise your weight.

TOM   Sit down.

> *DARRYL is very close to TOM, arms outstretched.*

DARRYL   Step up pussy, show me some skills.

TOM   Sit on the fucking chair.

> *DARRYL laughs.*

Shut up. Shut up you fucking

> *DARRYL laughs harder. TOM grabs DARRYL and manhandles him into the chair.*

sit on the chair. Sit on the fucking chair.

> *TOM holds DARRYL by the collar and shouts into his face.*

Freak. Fuck up. Fucking fuck up.

> *TOM breaks away from DARRYL.*

Fucking stupid fucking

> *He throws his own chair over, rubs his eyes and head.*

> *Silence. DARRYL freezes, staring at TOM.*

> ,

> *TOM looks at DARRYL.*

> ,

listen,

that was wrong.

> ,

You were winding me up and

DARRYL   I didn't think we used those kinda words Sir, man.

TOM   We don't. That was wrong of me. That was no way to behave.
           I'm sorry Darryl.

,

DARRYL   That was well funny.

,

TOM   You understand why I shouted, don't you Darryl?

DARRYL   Definitely.

TOM   Good.

DARRYL   'Cause you're mental.

TOM   No.

DARRYL   I thought I was a bit wacky but you is well bats.

TOM   It was wrong of me to

DARRYL   eccentric init?
Nutty professor.

TOM   Yeah, alright.

DARRYL   'Sit the fuck down!'

TOM   Yeah, okay. Let's laugh about it and forget I said anything.
Please Darryl, accept my apology. That was just, we just

conflict of personalities.

Alright?

TOM holds his hand out to DARRYL.

TOM   It's no way to behave and I'm

I wouldn't want you to think that I'm that kind of

,

I'm sorry. Alright?
Darryl?

,

DARRYL   Do you like me?

,

TOM   What?

TOM puts his hand back down.

DARRYL   Do you think I'm alright?

TOM   I

DARRYL   I think I'm alright.

          ,

TOM   You're alright.

DARRYL   That's what I reckoned.

TOM   A little irritating at times.

DARRYL   Is it?

TOM   At times.

DARRYL   Wind up.

          ,

TOM   So that's all forgotten then. What just happened is in the
          past.
          It's History. Alright?

          ,

DARRYL   Whatever.

          ,

TOM   Right. Good.
          Listen, forget about the project, let's do a few minutes
          work and you can do whatever you want on the
          computers.

          Alright?

DARRYL   Ain't we going on the computers now?

TOM   We need to do a little bit of work.

          DARRYL mutters to himself.

          Darryl?

DARRYL   You said ten minutes.

TOM   Ten minutes of work.

DARRYL   Gosh man.

TOM   Let's do five minutes.

> ,

DARRYL stands.

DARRYL   Nah. Fuck that.

TOM   Language.

DARRYL starts jogging on the spot.

DARRYL   Fuck your fucking language.

TOM   Sit down Darryl.

DARRYL   Fucking lying crazy fuck agency liar.

TOM   Darryl stop it.

DARRYL   Fuck your cunting slut fuck of a motherfucking bitch.

TOM   Darryl sit down.

DARRYL   Bet your woman's a whore init?

TOM   Shut up.

DARRYL   Real slosher.

TOM   Darryl stop it right now.

DARRYL   You're the fucking freak, freak boy.

TOM   Calm down.

DARRYL   You've given it your chat, I'm having my ikkle rant now, you get me?

TOM   Don't you want the gold sticker?

DARRYL   Fuck it. Fucking stickers.

> ,

TOM   Darryl, I'm going to call senior staff.

DARRYL runs towards TOM and jumps onto the table.

DARRYL   Call them. Fucking do it. Bring it on. You're wasting a man's time. You're wasting my fucking time here. What am I doing here? What's the point?

TOM   Get off the table.

DARRYL   Why?

TOM   Because I'm telling you.

DARRYL   And I'm telling you no.

TOM   Get. Down. Now.

DARRYL   My nan was right. You repping out like you're something special. Frontin' like you better than me. But you're just a fucking savage. Deep down and dirty you're just a gorilla.

TOM   Darryl, get off the

DARRYL   how's this for a project?
Let me on the computers
now
and I won't cut you, won't stick a fucking kitchen knife in your fucking eyes.

TOM   Get down.

DARRYL   Carve you up like a fucking animal.

TOM   Please Darryl, calm down.

DARRYL   Cover you in petrol and just watch you burn. Fucking screaming like a bitch.

TOM   Darryl. Sit on your chair.

DARRYL   Are you scared?

TOM   Darryl,

DARRYL   are you though?

TOM   Sit down now.

DARRYL starts to run on the spot on the table.

Darryl, get off the table.
Now.

DARRYL continues to run, increasingly fast. He starts to shout, a sound that rises and rises until he is bellowing at the top of his lungs.

Darryl.
Darryl get off the table.

Darryl, I'm telling you now to get down off the table.
Immediately.

Darryl.

,

4

Midday. School.

RITA sits at the table. She wears an angel brooch. She looks around her anxiously, clutching her handbag. On the table is a bunch of flowers wrapped in coloured paper.

'

TOM enters, holding a stack of papers which he places on the table face down.

TOM   Mrs Clark.

> *TOM holds out his hand for her to shake. RITA quickly shows him the palm of her hand and returns it to her bag.*

RITA   Yes, hello.

TOM   Sorry to keep you waiting.
Thanks for coming in.

RITA   I can't stay long. I'm on my way to church. Visit my daughter's grave every week at two.

TOM   I understand.

RITA   I'm not going to get a chance for lunch.

TOM   Really?

RITA   I thought this was probably more important.

TOM   Well, yes.

RITA   I'll grab a sandwich or something later.

TOM   Yes, good idea. I can hang your bag up for you if you like.

RITA   It's fine.
Actually, how long is this going to take?

TOM   Oh, it shouldn't be too
well,

no, it shouldn't take too long.

TOM sits.

RITA   Good.

TOM   Mrs Clark,

RITA   Rita.

TOM   Obviously this is about Darryl.

RITA   There's a Boots near the cemetery. They do sandwiches and things there I think.

TOM   Yes. Yes they do. I live up near there and I

TOM closes his eyes.

,

Mrs Clark,

He opens his eyes.

as you know, Darryl has been out of lessons officially for more than six months.

RITA   It's the Head of Year. She's got something against him.

TOM   Well, that's not actually

RITA   ego trip. Picking on him.

TOM   Mrs Clark, that's not

RITA   when is he going back into lessons?

TOM   Mrs Clark,

RITA   Rita.

TOM   I have concerns about Darryl.

RITA   You can't expel him.

TOM   That's not what I'm saying.

RITA   God help me I'll sue you. I'll fight you to keep him in this school. He's done nothing wrong.

TOM   I'm not saying that he has, I'm

RITA   he's no different to any of the other boys his age.

TOM   Actually, that's simply not

RITA   it's this school. This school has been nothing but trouble.

TOM   I'm just trying to do the best thing for him.

RITA   Bullying him.

'

TOM   I assure you that everyone here has Darryl's best interests at heart.

RITA   Really?

TOM   Yes. Absolutely.

RITA   They don't though, do they?

TOM   Yes,
yes, they absolutely do.

Mrs Clark, you have to understand that Darryl cannot be admitted to normal lessons.

RITA   You won't let him.

TOM   We can't. It's not fair on the other students. He is extremely disruptive. It's hard enough to just get him to

RITA   you saying I don't know my own grandson?

TOM   No.

RITA   I look after him as best I can.

TOM   Of course.

RITA   He'll work harder.

TOM   I don't think it's an issue of that.

RITA   Leave it with me. He'll work harder.

TOM   Mrs Clark, please, you're not listening to me.

RITA   Excuse me?

TOM   If you would just hear me out.

RITA   I don't appreciate that tone Mr

TOM   Tom. Just Tom, please.

RITA   Aren't you a proper teacher?

TOM   Yes. Yes, I am.
        I'm retraining.

RITA   Oh, that's just great. Poor kid's been fobbed off with everyone and their dog and now they bring in a student.

TOM   Mrs Clark,

RITA   aren't you a bit old to be training? What are you, thirty-odd?

TOM   I don't think it's your grandson's fault.

RITA   Of course it's not his fault. What are you talking about?

TOM   What I'm saying is, I don't think his behavioural problems are entirely his fault.
        I think he may have certain

        I think we could be doing more to help him.

RITA   I live for that boy.

TOM   Of course.

RITA   He has a good home.

TOM   The school tries to be as inclusive as possible, but it just we just don't have the resources. As much as we'd like to.

RITA   Here we go.

TOM   Mrs Clark, time is running out. As soon as Darryl turns fifteen his options rapidly diminish. He's then much more likely to fall into the judicial system than

RITA   you're talking another language.

TOM   It means he'll be dealt with by the police and not the school or doctors or

RITA   he's not ill.

TOM   No, but he might
        he might need special

RITA he's not crazy.

TOM That's not what I'm saying.

RITA It is though, isn't it?

,

TOM 'Crazy' isn't a helpful word.

RITA I don't believe this.

TOM I'd like to suggest that Darryl sees Dr Patterson. He works with many of the schools in the county and

RITA that's always the answer. Throw pills at it.

TOM It's not uncommon for

RITA his mother was drugged up to her eyeballs and ended up hanging from a coat hook.

TOM Mrs Clark,

RITA do you believe in God Mr

TOM Mrs Clark, please,

RITA after my daughter's death I was in a very dark place. I blamed myself. I was her mother

I was her mother and I hadn't been able to

> *RITA opens her bag and takes out a packet of tissues. She takes a tissue and blows her nose.*

the world is very cold when you live without hope. Do you understand that?

,

Now I have my angels. My belief gives me great strength. It fortifies me.

I can't say I've been convinced by doctors.

,

TOM Mrs Clark, I

I have hope.
For Darryl.

It's just
it's not just a case of

a number of students, for example, at this school have
ADHD, Attention Deficit and Hyperactivity

RITA   he's got one of those.

TOM   One of

RITA   he's not allowed in the town centre after he set fire to all
those bins.

TOM   Well, that's, no that's an ASBO, an Anti-Social Behaviour

RITA   it's all the same. Just a posh way of saying your kid's
messed up.

,

I'm not having him take tablets every day.

TOM   I'm not saying that medication would be the entire
solution, but we need to be realistic about

RITA   we tried him on Ritalin when he was eleven. Do you
know what it did to him? He was a zombie.

I must say I'm appalled. This school.

TOM   I'd like to suggest that Darryl goes part-time at the school.
I can help to arrange for a counsellor to visit him at your
home and work with him on

RITA   when will he be going back to lessons?

,

TOM   Mrs Clark, I'm very concerned about the kind of films
Carl has been allowing Darryl to watch.

,

RITA   What?

TOM Darryl has seen a number of very graphic films which he has led me to understand have been purchased for him by your
partner.

>*RITA stands.*

RITA I don't believe this.

>*TOM stands.*

TOM You understand why it would be a concern.

RITA Carl doesn't know what these films are. Darryl says what he wants and Carl gets it for him.

>*RITA looks down.*

,

It's hard to say no to him.
Anything we can do to keep him quiet.

TOM A lot of these videos simply aren't appropriate.

RITA Every other kid has seen these movies.

TOM That may be, but Darryl has particularly little empathy and a fascination
no
obsession
with violence and torture.

RITA He's a fourteen-year-old boy.

>*TOM turns the stack of papers over and spreads the pages across the desk. RITA looks at them.*

>*Silence.*

TOM Darryl had been using the Internet during final period yesterday. This morning when I turned the printer on, this is what came out.

RITA That doesn't prove anything.

TOM I checked the history on his Internet account.

,

RITA   Where were you? Why was he left unsupervised?

TOM   As much as we try to, we can't watch him every second.
        And I can't be in all day every day, so he's left with a
        member of senior staff who have their own work to do.

        RITA looks at the papers.

RITA   What is all this?

TOM   I'm sorry. I had hoped I wouldn't have to show you these.

,

RITA   Oh gosh.

TOM   This is just some of what he was looking at yesterday.
        There are some pictures which I thought were too
        harrowing
        to include.

RITA   What do you expect? If this stuff is so easy to find on the
        computer then of course it's going to be looked at.

TOM   We have software to block certain searches, but there are
        ways round it.

RITA   None of this means anything. He's just curious.

TOM   These pictures aren't pretend. They're not from films or

        they're real people. Real bruises, and burns and cuts and

RITA   Darryl doesn't know that. He doesn't know the difference.

TOM   That might be true, but

RITA   I've seen enough.

TOM   Mrs Clark, not every fourteen-year-old boy wants to see
        these images.

RITA   You can't deny my grandchild an education.

        *TOM singles out a particular piece of paper and hands it to
        RITA. She looks at it and covers her mouth with her hand.*

,

Dear God.

TOM   I'm sorry you have to see this. Particularly because your
        daughter

how she

,

but it's important that you know.

It's important that you know what is occupying his mind.

,

Listen, Mrs Clark, this would be more than reason enough
to expel Darryl. But, so far, I haven't shown this to anyone
else.

I don't believe that expulsion would be the best thing for
him. Do you?

,

RITA shakes her head.

It would mean more disruption and wasted time and

I think we can really help him. We need to agree that
something needs to be done, then start working with
Dr Patterson. If we act quickly we can avoid not only
expulsion but put systems in place to stop him doing
something really

RITA   he's haunted.

There's something

there's still something lurking under his bed.
I hear him talking at night.

He
wets the bed.

He still wets the bed. I can't stand it.
He'll be fifteen soon and

I can't

,

I told him I won't deal with it anymore.

I just let him lie in it.
I'm

his room stinks. I don't go in there.

,

A knife's gone from my kitchen.

TOM   Mrs Clark, one-to-one supervision alone isn't working.

RITA   He's not leaving this school.

TOM   If anyone else in the staff knew about this there wouldn't
be a choice, there would be nothing I could do.

,

I'm trying to do the right thing.

,

If you want him to stay five days a week at the school,
then medication will be unavoidable. And if that didn't
work then we'll have wasted valuable time. All that will be
left is specialist residential schools or

and neither of us want it to come to that.

RITA is looking at the paper in her hand.

,

RITA   What's the doctor's name?

5

School. Lunch-time. Children are playing loudly outside.

DARRYL is sat at the table, writing. TOM is stood behind him, looking at his work.

Silence.

TOM   You can stop writing now.

    Silence.

Do you want a break?

Darryl?

    ,

    TOM looks at DARRYL's bag on the hook.

    ,

You've been working for a few hours. It's break time.

Do you want to go out? Have a run around?

It is your birthday.

    ,

Darryl?

Football?

    ,

Darryl, your mates are out there. Kieran's out there.

    DARRYL looks up towards the door, wearily.

    Silence.

    He looks back down again.

Darryl?

    ,

How are you feeling since seeing the doctor?

DARRYL shrugs.

,

DARRYL   He axed me about Mum.

,

TOM   Yeah?

DARRYL   And Carl. Lots of questions about Carl.
And Dad.

,

TOM   What did he ask you about Carl?

,

Darryl, is there something you should

DARRYL   nah. Carl's alright.

,

TOM   What have you written?

Can I read it?

*DARRYL shrugs. TOM takes the exercise book from in front of
DARRYL and turns back a few pages.*

,

(*Reads.*) Dog,
by Darryl Clark.

TOM smiles at DARRYL.

My dog is called

what's that word?

,

DARRYL   Swastika.

It's like a cross. Bit spastic. Squished spider.
See it all over round our way.
Back a yard people been using it as their tag.

Nan knows what it is.

,

TOM   My dog is called Swastika.
He's bigger than a puppy but not as big as a grown-up
dog.

> *TOM looks up at DARRYL. DARRYL is staring at the floor. TOM
> looks back at the work.*

One day we were playing and Swastika was jumping up at
me and I was pushing him away and each time I pushed
him he'd bounce back harder and show his teeth so I'd
push him harder and he'd keep

this is a long sentence Darryl, you can break this up.

> *TOM makes some marks with his pen.*

He'd keep jumping up at me and then I shoved him and
his back leg twisted

his back leg twisted and he
can't read that word.

DARRYL   Yelped.

TOM   And he yelped and looked at me and

,

DARRYL   snarled.

TOM   And tried to bite me so I
smacked him
and it hurt my hand and he barked and I kicked him and
he kept coming at me and I kept boxing him and I got
blood on my hands that was his and my knuckles all split
open
and he kept coming at me and panting with his tongue out
that he'd bit into and his eyes glaring at me and he kept
coming and he was snapping and barking and I barked
back.

And I barked back.

,

TOM looks up at DARRYL.

Is this true Darryl?
Did you ever kick a dog?

,

I'm going to have another chat with your nan and suggest
that we apply for a place for you at Greenacres. It's a
school, much like this one, but it's residential, which
means that you'd have your own room and
it's better equipped to deal with
I mean to

it would be better for you there.

DARRYL   Will I still be able to do GCSEs?

,

TOM   Darryl, you've not been in classes for almost

DARRYL   if I don't get GCSEs how will I get a job?

,

TOM   Darryl, I'm sorry, but this school isn't the best place for
you. I'm just thinking about
about what's best for you.

How would you feel about moving somewhere else?

,

DARRYL shrugs.

,

*TOM looks back at the book. He turns the page, scan-reading
for a moment.*

Swastika dropped back to the floor, dragging my arm
with him and ripping it open. Red everywhere. Dark. I
stamped on him and felt a crack.

He was panting and whining and I was crying.

TOM *looks up at* DARRYL.

I took his jaw in my hands and twisted it round until his neck crunched and he stopped.
I stood in the living-room without moving and watched the little bits of black fur in the air.

,

Did this happen Darryl?
It's very vivid. Very descriptive.

Did you hurt a dog Darryl?

,

DARRYL   Nah.

I killed a baby rabbit when I was a kid.

Nan won't let me have a dog.

,

TOM   You've worked really hard today Darryl.

I think you've earned a sticker, don't you?
Would you like to choose one?

,

Darryl?

,

Interval.

6

Evening. House.

TOM sits at the table wearing a black suit. JODI sits on his knee, wearing pyjamas and a wedding veil. They have their hands on her belly.

A bottle of champagne and two tall glasses sit on the table.

,

JODI   This thing.
This

monster.

,

I'm a house.
I'm a big flesh balloony home for a creature I don't know.

Life-support system.
My heart pumping into another. Little tiny

sharing my food. Giving me backache. Changing my moods.

Growing.
Listening.

Silence.

How can I get any bigger?
How can I have another eight weeks?

,

TOM takes her hand gently in his and kisses it. She smiles.

,

TOM   You're crushing me.

They smile. He helps her up and stands, staring into space. She leans against the table and watches him.

,

JODI   Husband.

>*TOM smiles.*

>Incredibly odd word.
>Husband.

>Hus
>band.

>,

>Wife.

>I'm a wife.

>a
>wife.

TOM   You shouldn't have got drunk.

JODI   It's my wedding day.

TOM   You shouldn't have been drinking.

JODI   It's my wedding day and I'm a blimp.

TOM   Jodi, I'm serious.

JODI   Don't start.

TOM   I'm not.

JODI   Don't.

TOM   I just don't want it to

JODI   don't you dare.

TOM   I want it to be

>no problems.

JODI   It will be. It will.

>*JODI looks at TOM.*

>,

>How are you feeling?

>,

TOM   Wonderful.

JODI   Really?

TOM   I've just married my soulmate. My best friend.
        Why wouldn't I be happy?

                ,

JODI   I'm worried about you.

TOM   I know.

JODI   You're not going to want to go back.

TOM   That's certainly true.

JODI   You should quit.

                ,

TOM   You're probably right.

JODI   But you won't.

                ,

TOM   I can't believe that she doesn't want what's best for her
        own grandson.

JODI   Let's not talk about it.
        Not today.

TOM   She hates the school but doesn't want him moved.

JODI   Of course she wants what's best.

TOM   Greenacres is fine. It's got staff who are properly trained
        to deal with kids who are
        you know, students who are

JODI   crazy?
        Loony? Mental?

TOM   Stop it.

JODI   Mad? Bonkers?

TOM   It's not funny.

,

Sorry.
It's just not.

JODI   I know.

TOM   I don't know what I'd do if this one is born

JODI   don't

TOM   born with

JODI   please.

,

TOM   I can't stop thinking about it.

JODI   No.
I know.

,

TOM   He can't help it.

JODI   Poor thing.

TOM   It's chemical.

JODI   And bad parenting.

TOM   Well,

JODI   isn't it?

,

TOM   I don't know what I'd be like. If we had
if our kid was

but we'd still want what's best for him.

JODI   Yes. Of course.

TOM   We'd still make sure he was getting the best support and
care.

JODI   Or her.

TOM   Eating the right food.

JODI   Tom.

TOM   I'm a vampire.

JODI   No.

TOM   All those years I spent at that company. Working out new ways to get kids to consume expensive colourful garbage.

JODI   Tom,

TOM   that last project, targeting children's cancer wards and getting them to install vending machines full of

JODI   Tom stop it.

That's all bullshit anyway. That's not why you quit.

That's not why you

,

seriously sweetheart, who are you talking to?

,

You didn't do anything wrong.
And even if you did, you're making up for it.

,

TOM   Still.

We've created a whole generation of
a whole generation that can't feed themselves.

JODI   He isn't the way he is because of what he's eaten.

TOM   That's not what I'm saying.

JODI   You can't punish yourself.

TOM   Not just the food but everything. It's all colourful and disposable and bad for you. Just listening to him speak is like
everything he knows he's got from TV, American TV, and it's all lies. And then we persecute him because he doesn't know how to get on in the real world.

JODI   There must be some hope for him. He's a child, he's not a

TOM   I know.

JODI   Aren't most of these kids really good at maths or something?

TOM   What do you mean, these kids?

JODI   Don't shout at me.

TOM   I'm not shouting Jodi, but seriously you can't just

TOM gestures and JODI flinches.

'

what's that?

'

You just flinched.

JODI   No.

TOM   Shit.

JODI   Stop it.

TOM   Why the fuck are you flinching? What do you think I'm

JODI starts clearing the table.

JODI   stop it.

TOM   Stop what? What the fuck am I

JODI   calm down, please.

TOM   I'm calm I'm

you still don't trust me.

Oh fuck.
You still don't trust me.

I'd never
what happened before,
I'd never again

I'd never hurt you.

JODI   I'm sorry.

TOM   Oh fuck.

JODI   Listen, Tom I'm sorry. I'm tired.

TOM   I'm fine. I'm fine now. I'm doing something I care about and

JODI   I know.

TOM   Oh shit.

JODI   Forget about it. It was just a nervous reaction.

TOM   Jodi.

JODI   I'm jumpy. Like you said.
My moods, I'm

hey, I'm fine. I'm sorry.

TOM   You're really worried I might be losing it?

,

Listen, it's pressure, but it's not the same kind of
I'd never

I'm not losing it.
I'm not losing it.

I

,

JODI sits at the table.

JODI   so he isn't good at maths, is that what you're saying?

She tops up her glass.

,

TOM   No.

JODI   And even with a better mum and dad he still wouldn't be?

,

TOM   I don't think so.

,

JODI   So whose fault is it?

,

TOM   No one's.

,

JODI   So what hope is there?

,

TOM   If I can get him into this place

JODI   Greenacres.

TOM   Get him into Greenacres and then there's hope.

JODI   But you got him a place.

TOM   Yes.

JODI   They're happy to take him.

TOM   Yes.

JODI   So what's the problem?

,

TOM   It's up to his nan.

JODI   Oh. Yes, you said.

        JODI rubs her eyes.

TOM   Otherwise

,

JODI   otherwise what?

,

TOM   I have this horrible feeling.

        I just can't help feeling that one day
        he's going to

JODI   what?

,

TOM   He's got zero empathy. You could be having a conversation and start choking to death and he'd just think 'well, this conversation's over'.

He'd probably just sit there and finish eating whatever you were choking on.

I can't do anything.

JODI   Then quit.

TOM   I can't.

JODI   Transfer schools.
If you're serious.

Tom, listen,
please.
It's sweet that you care. I love you for it. But I'm asking you, please, to stop it.
For me.

You've got a family now.

TOM   Do you know how many teachers Darryl has had since they kicked him out of proper lessons?

JODI   That's not your problem.

TOM   I've a responsibility.

JODI   You've got a responsibility to me.

TOM   I just want to do something

you know what I mean.
I've got the chance to really

everything I read or watch tells me that I don't care or that I'm
you know, I'm apathetic or

and I'm sick of it.
I'm not. I'm not apathetic.

I just don't know what to do.

There's a difference.

TOM looks at JODI.

,

What happened in the city

I don't understand what happened and
I

but
if it leads to something good. If it means that this lost kid
gets to

a better life

then

JODI looks away from TOM.

,

alright, say it. Say what you need to say. I'm listening.
Let's have the conversation. If you tell me to quit, if you
seriously tell me to just quit then I'll do it. Give me an
ultimatum. Say it. Tell me. Tell me that you want me to

JODI   it wasn't an accident.

,

I wanted to have a baby.

,

I don't want to be alone in this big house. I want it filled
with children. I want to hear little voices laughing. I want
a family.

,

And I've had to do this all on my own.
And I'm terrified.

I'm hanging by a thread.

And this student is of no relevance to me. He's nothing.
From where I'm standing he is of zero fucking importance.

,

TOM   I'm sorry it's got to me so much.

JODI   It's all you've been able to talk about.

TOM   I know. I'm sorry.

JODI   I'm going through something myself.

TOM   Alright.

JODI   He's just a fucked up kid. You can't save them all. There's
       millions.

       And you're not doing it for him. You're doing it to make
       yourself feel better and that's selfish and stupid.

TOM   Fine. Alright. I'm sorry.

JODI   You're having a child of your own.

TOM   I know.

JODI   You're never here. You keep escaping.

TOM   I'm not escaping.

JODI   Going for walks or

TOM   I'm not

JODI   even when you're here, you're never completely

TOM   okay. Okay, I'm sorry.

JODI   I need you.
       I need you to
       I need you to hold my hand.

       ,

       We've just got to hope that this one isn't a nutter.

TOM   Yes.

JODI   And if it is

TOM   don't.

JODI   If it is,

we'll just have to love it even more.

,

TOM   I know I haven't said, but
        having this child is

        to have a family
        with you

        never knowing my real parents,
        there's a huge part of my history that I don't feel I

        to have that with you
        to look at a child and know that it's mine
        my own

        that scares me to death.

        ,

        I can't quit Jo.
        I have to just see this through. Get him into this residential
        place and then I won't be needed at the school.
        I'll be all yours.

        ,

JODI   Okay.

        Listen,
        soon he'll be gone and it won't be your problem.

        JODI touches her stomach.

TOM   What?

        ,

JODI   I think I just felt it kick.

7

Night. RITA's house. There are angel figurines around the room.

Rain.

RITA is crying. She is bleeding from her head and very shaken.

RITA And then he came at me.

TOM Where is he now?

RITA His eyes.

Just tiny black dots in the white. Cruel, angry

TOM Rita, listen to me.

RITA I'm shaking. I'm sorry.

TOM Rita, where is Darryl?

RITA I'm sorry I called you.

TOM It's fine.
Rita,

RITA I didn't think, it's

what,

it must be four in the morning.

TOM You did the right thing.

RITA I couldn't call the police.

TOM No.

RITA Not on my own grandson.

TOM I understand.

RITA What kind of person would that make me?

TOM Rita, did Darryl not take his medication?

RITA I don't know.

TOM   Rita, this is very

RITA   I don't know, I leave it to him. It's been fine, he's been
       fine so I've left it to him this past few weeks. See how he'd
       get on.

       You've been away.

              ,

TOM   Alright.
       Alright.

       Rita, where is Darryl?

RITA   I'm so scared.

TOM   Where is he?

RITA   Upstairs.

              ,

       TOM looks up.

       What are you going to do?

              ,

TOM   How long has he been up there?

RITA   When did I call you?

TOM   About

RITA   he was up there then, banging around. I heard breaking.

TOM   When did everything go quiet?

RITA   About

TOM   do you think he's hurt himself?

RITA   Oh.

TOM   Is it possible?

RITA   I hadn't thought.

TOM   Did he take the knife with him?

RITA   Oh no.

TOM   Rita. Where is the knife now?

RITA   I

         ,

TOM   alright. Listen,
         are you sure you're not hurt?

RITA   Bleeding but
         no. Just shaken.

TOM   Okay. Call an ambulance. Just in case he's

         I'll

         TOM stares at the ceiling.

         ,

         listen, Rita,
         I'm sorry,

         I can't

         my wife is pregnant. She's got five weeks.

         ,

         I can't go up there.

         I'm sorry. I

         she'd never forgive me.

RITA   He'll listen to you.

TOM   I'm just his teacher.

         I can't risk my child growing up without a father.

         There is a loud crash above them.

         ,

RITA   Is it your first?

         ,

TOM   Yes.

RITA   Boy or girl?

TOM   We don't know. We didn't want to know until

           Rita, Darryl needs to be at a residential school.

RITA   Talk to him. Please.

TOM   I really don't think

RITA   you have to.
           I can't

           I can't do this on my own.
           I can't do it anymore.

TOM   I know.

RITA   What's got into him?

TOM   Rita, at Greenacres there are trained, professional people who can

RITA   no.

TOM   Darryl needs to be

RITA   you don't understand.

TOM   No, I don't. I don't understand.
           What will it take to make you

RITA   I just want him to have a normal life, go to a normal school.

TOM   Of course, but

RITA   he's my daughter's son.

TOM   I know. I know that Mrs Clark but

RITA   he found her.

           ,

           She didn't pick him up from school. He walked home and found her in the living-room.

           The coat hanger had cut into her throat. Her whole face was dark blue, eyes wide open.

           He was so little.

,

I can't fail him.
I can't fail my daughter.

,

More sounds from above.

,

TOM   Keeping him at the school is not fair on him Rita.

I'm just trying to do what's best.

,

RITA   Yes.

TOM   Greenacres will take him.
You don't have to do this on your own anymore.

,

RITA   If you talk to him.
If you talk to him, then

,

then okay.

,

A loud crash. They look up.

8

Morning. School. Bright sunshine streaming through the windows.

Children playing outside.

TOM is sat at the table.

,

DARRYL enters. He drops his bag on the floor.

DARRYL   Boom!

TOM   Darryl.

DARRYL   A'ight agency.

TOM   Tom.

DARRYL   Yeah, yeah. Tom.

TOM   You can call me Tom you know Darryl. You've not done up until now you may as well on your last day.

You said goodbye to your friends?

DARRYL   Yeah.
Yeah we had a gathering.

TOM   Did you?

DARRYL   Going away party. A rave.

TOM   Good.

DARRYL   Believe. Some tunes. Some bitches.
It was heavy. Me bleach *hard.*

TOM   Right.

DARRYL   Cristal. Celebrities.

You should've come. Was pure fiyah. Solid. Hyphy. You get me?

TOM   Sorry I missed it.

DARRYL   It was off the hook.
         Could've brought your gyal.

TOM   My

DARRYL   your woman. Girlfriend, whatever.

TOM   Actually, she's my wife now Darryl.
         We got married last month.

                ,

DARRYL   Your wife. Whatever. You could've brung her.

         DARRYL sits down.

TOM   Maybe next time.

DARRYL   F'shizzle ma nizzle.
         Can I axe you a question?

TOM   Darryl, sit on your chair properly.

DARRYL   Can I though?

TOM   What do you want to know?

DARRYL   I bet you got a well nice house init?

TOM   Why do you ask?

DARRYL   Nan saw you up at the cemetery init? Saw you coming
         out of one of those big houses. Dem old ones. Lakeside
         Mansions.

TOM   It's alright.

DARRYL   Is it a mansion though? Proper massive manor?

TOM   No. No, it's actually

DARRYL   fountains and limousines and shit.

         TOM laughs.

TOM   No.

DARRYL   Bet you can see the lake though init?

                ,

TOM   From the top bedroom you can see the far west corner of
           the lake.

DARRYL   Reckon I'll have a view in this new place?

TOM   You looking forward to going?

           ,

DARRYL   Yeah.
           Yeah, it'll be a'ight.

TOM   It'll be much better for you at Greenacres than here.

DARRYL   Yeah. It'll be good init?

           Had a look around.

           ,

           Dem's all spazzas init?

TOM   All the students have certain specific

DARRYL   spastications.

TOM   No, they are all

DARRYL   retarded.

TOM   No.

DARRYL   They are though init?

TOM   No.

DARRYL   Except they are though.

           TOM smiles, despite himself.

           ,

           Gonna be in with the ruffnicks init?

           ,

TOM   I'm sure it won't be too bad.

DARRYL   Yeah. Whatever.

TOM   How's the new meds?

DARRYL   Yeah. I'm taking them if that's what you're asking.

TOM   Good. Good.
And you're not as drowsy? Not as out-of-it?

DARRYL   I's on this planet bruv.

TOM   Glad to hear it.

DARRYL   Focused, you get me?
It's like your shoes.

TOM looks at his shiny black shoes.

TOM   What about my shoes?

DARRYL   Brand new brand new. Wicked steez. Spic and span, y'get me?

TOM   Right.

DARRYL   In your case though, they just make everything else look cheap init?

TOM   Do they?

DARRYL   Classy shoes, granddad trousers.

TOM   So you're feeling alright?

DARRYL   Superstar.

TOM   Great.
Keep taking them.

DARRYL   You got it brah.

TOM   Good.

,

DARRYL   What about you?

,

TOM   What about me?

DARRYL   If I'm gone then your project's over init?

TOM   Yeah. Yeah, that's right.

DARRYL   Your last day an' all.

TOM   That's it.

> *Silence. They look at one another. TOM smiles, DARRYL stares at him.*

DARRYL   So, that it?
Can I go now?

> ,

TOM   Well, it's early, but,
yeah. Go on.

> ,

DARRYL   Bless up.

> *DARRYL stands.*

> ,

I'm sorry about that time I called you a monkey.

> ,

TOM   Gorilla.

DARRYL   Yeah. Yeah.

> ,

TOM   Goodbye Darryl.
Look after yourself. Alright?

> ,

DARRYL   Yeah.
Yeah. Peace.

> ,

> *TOM watches DARRYL leave.*

> ,

9

Night. House.

JODI enters, carrying a bottle of wine and a large glass. She is heavily pregnant.

She stands at the table, takes the cork out of the bottle and fills her glass. She looks at her watch then stares towards the door.

She nurses the glass with both hands and takes a sip. She stares at it.

,

She takes a big swig.

,

She drains the glass.

The doorbell rings. She puts the glass on the table.

JODI It's open babes.

    She exits to the kitchen.

    ,

    DARRYL enters.

    He looks around. His eyes are wide.

(*Off.*) You're back early.
How was today?

I was just about to eat without you.
I would've waited but,
when you gotta eat, you gotta eat.

But at least I'm awake. Sorry about the last few nights.
Sorry about the sofa. I just can't get back to sleep once I wake up.

You know.

I packed my suitcase today ready for

JODI enters, carrying a plate of food and some cutlery. She sees DARRYL and freezes.

Silence.

hello.

DARRYL	Alright?
JODI	Are you with Tom?

,

DARRYL	Is Tom here?
JODI	He's not here?
DARRYL	Is that a question?

,

JODI	Sorry. He he must still be

perhaps you could come back another time.
Or better yet, do you have the number?

DARRYL	Telephone.
JODI	Just give us a bell later in the week and
DARRYL	nah, nah. Wanted to see the man in person, you get me?

She places the plate and cutlery on the table. She is very frightened.

JODI	Are you his student?
DARRYL	When's he back?
JODI	He should be back any minute.
DARRYL	Cool. I'll wait.

,

JODI	I didn't get your name.
DARRYL	Didn't get it.

JODI   No.

DARRYL   Nah.

JODI   I'm Jodi.

DARRYL   Yeah, yeah.

Darryl.
You got a well nice crib init?

JODI   Thing is Darryl, it's very late and
as you can see
I'm

DARRYL   yeah.
You're massive.
Up the duff init?

Gonna be a mum.

,

JODI   Yeah.
So I think you should just come back another time.

,

Alright?

DARRYL   Can you see the lake from your bedroom?

,

JODI   No.

DARRYL   I think you can.

,

JODI   Will you please leave?

DARRYL   Once I seen the lake init?

,

JODI   Get out please.

DARRYL   You being moody?
You picking a fight?

JODI   No.

DARRYL   Because I don't think that's wise, do you?

JODI   I'm not picking a fight.

DARRYL   State you're in.

JODI   I'm sorry, I didn't mean

          ,

          would you like something to drink?

DARRYL   Trying to get me drunk?

JODI   No.

DARRYL   You are though init?

JODI   I'm definitely not.

DARRYL   Except you are though. Dutty gyal.

JODI   Are you hungry?
          Why don't you wait for Tom? Sit down. Have something
          to eat.

DARRYL   Ain't hungry.

JODI   Watch TV then?

          ,

DARRYL   You got any DVDs?

JODI   We've got some videos.

DARRYL   Can I see the lake?

JODI   It'll be too dark now, you won't be able to see anything.

DARRYL   Won't see anything?

JODI   It's pitch black.

DARRYL   It is well dark init?

JODI   Tom's thinking of getting a little boat. You should call up
          in a few weeks and maybe Tom'll take you out on it.

          ,

DARRYL   What videos you got?

>   *JODI is moving slowly towards the table.*

JODI   What kind of thing do you want to watch?

DARRYL   Do you like me?

>   ,

JODI   I don't know you.

DARRYL   Is it?

JODI   I'm sure you're very nice.

DARRYL   You're sure.

JODI   As I say, I don't know you.

DARRYL   As you say.
       You trying to pick up that knife?

>   ,

JODI   No.

DARRYL   What you want that for?

JODI   Nothing. I wasn't.

DARRYL   You wanna slice me up?

JODI   No.

DARRYL   Gonna cut me is it?

JODI   I wasn't.

DARRYL   Slice my throat?

>   *DARRYL mimes his throat being cut, making a loud ripping noise. JODI is too frightened to speak.*

>   ,

       Have you got 'Pearl Harbour'?
       It's well good.

       Skip the chapters for about an hour anyway. First part's shit.

,

Pick it up.

JODI   Hmm?

DARRYL   The knife. Pick it up.

,

JODI   No.

DARRYL   Go on.

JODI   Now listen to me, if you don't leave now I'm going to call
            the police.

DARRYL   Is it?

JODI   Yes.

DARRYL   And say what?

JODI   Just
            I'll just ask them to remove you from my property.

DARRYL   Is it?

JODI   So please leave.

DARRYL   Pick it up.

JODI   No.

DARRYL   Pick it up.

JODI   No.

DARRYL   It's well poxy.
            Ikkle fing. Bet it's blunt as fuck.
            Come over here.

            JODI shakes her head.

            Silence.

            Look at this.

            *He unzips his bag and pulls out a large carving knife with
            a serrated blade.*

It's my nan's. It's excellent.

Have a look at it.

JODI shakes her head.

Don't you like me?

JODI   Please

DARRYL   please. Please.

You look a bit like my mum.
Like how she used to look.

Your hair and that.

,

JODI   What do you want?

,

DARRYL   Can you put your arm around my shoulder?

,

JODI   Alright.

,

DARRYL drops his bag on the floor and walks towards JODI, still holding the knife.

She puts her arms around him. He puts his free arm around her.

,

Alright Darryl.

DARRYL starts to cry.

Sssh.
It's okay Darryl.

Sssh.

Sssh.

Sssh.

Darryl,

why don't you put the knife down on the table?

Why don't you give me the knife?

> *DARRYL looks at her.*

DARRYL You want it?

JODI Yes.

DARRYL You want me to give you the knife?

> ,

JODI Yes.

> ,

DARRYL Okay.

> ,

> *He hands it to her, she takes it and puts it on the table.*

JODI Thank you Darryl.

> ,

> *Still embracing him, she looks at her watch, then to the door.*

> ,

DARRYL I've got to go back to my nan's.

JODI Yes. Good.

DARRYL It's well past curtain time.

JODI She'll be worried.

DARRYL I'll just look at the lake and go.

> *JODI closes her eyes.*

> ,

JODI Alright.

DARRYL Come on.

JODI   It's through the kitchen, up the stairs and straight ahead.

DARRYL   After you.

JODI   I'm alright here.

DARRYL   Ladies first.

JODI   I can't really

DARRYL   yes you can.

DARRYL picks up the knife.

JODI   Listen, please

DARRYL   no.

JODI   Please.

I'm due in eleven days. I'll just wait here and

DARRYL   do you think I'm stupid?

JODI   No.

I don't think you are.

DARRYL   You're well scared init?

JODI   Please.

DARRYL is smiling.

DARRYL   Are you going to piss yourself?

JODI is crying.

You were going to knife me init?

JODI shakes her head. She is too scared to speak.

Nah. Nah.
You're just scared init?

'

JODI nods. She has tears in her eyes.

'

Yeah. Me too.

,

JODI   Get out of my house.

Get out.
Now.

   DARRYL stares at JODI.

Get out of my fucking house.

,

I don't like you Darryl. I hate you. I don't want to bring
my baby into a world with you in it.

,

Why are you standing there?
What do you want?

I can't help you.
I'm sorry that you've been fucked around by your school.
I'm sorry that the whole education system is fucked, but
you know what? Most people cope with it. I'm sorry
you've seen lots of nasty films and been lied to and fed
bad food and gangster rap. I'm sorry that you blame
yourself for your father leaving and your mother killing
herself, and I'd like to say that it's not your fault but

it is. I'm sure neither of them could stand you.

I'm sorry that you've got nothing to look forward to.

But I'm not going to stand here and be intimidated by a
stupid, ugly, messed-up little boy.

Because of you I've barely had a moment to speak to
my husband during my whole pregnancy. I'm alone
and terrified and I don't need this. I'm at the end of my
patience.

So get out.
Now.

I'm going upstairs to call the police. I suggest you leave.

'

JODI exits.

Silence.

DARRYL picks up his bag and stands still, looking at the door.

Silence.

He looks in the direction JODI left.

'

He walks to the table and stands looking at the plate of food.

10

Graveyard. Lunch-time. Bird-song.

TOM sits on a bench, his head in his hands.

Silence.

RITA enters holding a plastic carrier-bag and a bunch of flowers. She doesn't see TOM. She walks to a small gravestone beside which is a small porcelain angel and some flowers, identical to those RITA is carrying but a week old. She crosses herself and stands for a moment staring at the stone.

TOM watches her.

RITA kneels and replaces the flowers, putting the old ones in the plastic bag. She spends a moment arranging the fresh ones.

,

She stands, with difficulty, brushes herself down and picks up the plastic bag. She turns towards the bench and sees TOM looking at her.

,

TOM   Mrs Clark.

,

I'm sorry, I didn't mean to

I didn't want to disturb you.

,

I live just up the road.
I come out here sometimes. Get out of the house.

,

Would you sit down?

,

RITA sits on the bench, as far from TOM as she can.

,

I think spring's coming. Mild today.
It'll be summer before we know it.

,

How are you? Are you well?

RITA   That's my daughter's grave.

TOM   I know. I'm sorry, I

RITA   did you follow me here?

,

TOM   I live just over the way.

RITA   Getting some fresh air.

TOM   Yes.
         Just

,

my wife is
she's asleep. She's been up all night with the baby.
They're getting some rest.

,

RITA   Boy or girl?

,

TOM   Boy.

,

*RITA opens her plastic bag and takes out a packet of
sandwiches, opens them and starts to eat.*

,

It's so quiet here. There's nowhere in the city this
peaceful.
Good place to just sit and think.

RITA   Escape the family. Get some peace and quiet.

,

TOM   I'm not escaping.

RITA   Oh.

TOM   I'm not escaping.

I often come down here with Howie, my son. Give my wife a break.

Silence.

Rita,

How's Darryl?

,

How's he getting on at the home?

RITA   It's not a home.

TOM   The secure child's home.

RITA   It's a remand centre. Borstal with a posh name. It's a nightmare.

He's much worse since he's been there.

,

They barely let me see him.

,

He wants to go back to school.

TOM   Right.

RITA   Do his exams.

TOM   Yeah.

RITA   They won't let him.

,

They can't decide if he's crazy or just

if they should keep him locked up or

,

he's a *child*.

,

Greenacres don't want him now.

,

I worry about him.

,

TOM   Mrs Clark,
        Rita,

        I heard there'd been a fire.

        At the home.
        I heard that part of the home had burnt down and

        ,

        I just wanted to know if he was alright.

RITA   You wanted to know if he'd done it.

        ,

TOM   Where is he now?

        Is he back with you?

        ,

RITA   Do you want the other half of this sandwich? I shan't eat it.

TOM   Rita?

RITA   Mexican Chicken.

TOM   I'm fine thanks.

RITA   Well it's there if you want it.

TOM   Rita, where is Darryl?

RITA   You still teaching?

        ,

TOM No.
No, me and Jodi, my wife,
we're going back to the city.
I'm going back to my old job.

RITA I thought you were here to apologise.

,

TOM Apologise for what?

RITA Darryl was let down by that school.
He was betrayed.
Particularly by you.

You let him down. Turned him into a

,

but I've forgiven you.

,

TOM Mrs Clark

RITA Rita.

,

TOM My wife

my wife could have been

it's lucky she didn't

,

whatever they decide, I think it's too late for Darryl. I
can't see any hope for him. He's a mess. He's

unfixable.

If he didn't start this fire, he'll start the next one.
He'll never go back to school. Never sit exams. Never
have a job.
He'll spend his life in and out of institutions.
Psychiatric hospitals. Prisons.

And there's nothing we can do but shake our heads.
Nothing.

,

I sometimes think
and I hate myself for it
but I sometimes think we should just take them all, all
the Darryls of this world and lock them in a room. Give
them all the knives and guns and matches they want and
let them sort it out amongst themselves. Drown them in
petrol.

I think what your daughter did was a terrible shame. What
she put you through and what she condemned Darryl to.
But someone like her shouldn't have been allowed to have
children. She should have been sterilised.
It's not fair on Darryl and it's not fair on anyone else.

My child has to live in this world.

Darryl is a fucking virus. Do you understand me?
I lie awake at night listening out for him. Knowing he's
out there.

My wife barely leaves the house.

Soon you'll be under the ground somewhere in here and
then what will happen to him?

,

RITA   Perhaps he should just be more like you.

,

> *Children shouting nearby. RITA looks over towards the
> school.*

,

Break time.

,

I wanted to be buried in here, but I don't think I will now.
It's full up.

I'll be in the new place over the other side of town.
By the motorway.

,

She looks back at TOM.

,

I love my grandson.

,

Go on. Have the other half.

,

TOM takes the sandwich. They sit and eat. RITA takes a packet of crisps from the bag and opens them. She offers the packet to TOM and he takes one.

,

TOM   Thanks.

,

JODI enters, carrying Howie, a sleeping baby. She stands watching TOM and RITA. TOM sees her.

,

JODI   I came to find you.

TOM   You were sleeping.

,

This is Mrs Clark.

RITA   Rita.

,

JODI   Hello.

,

TOM stands.

TOM   You were sleeping.

JODI   Woke up.

    ,

TOM   How is he?

JODI   Alright.

He's been screaming.

    ,

I don't really know what I'm doing.

RITA smiles politely at JODI. JODI smiles cautiously back.

    ,

TOM   It was good to see you again Rita.

RITA holds her hand out to TOM. He looks at it.

    ,

He takes her hand and shakes it.

    ,

Thanks for the sandwich.

RITA   Take care.

It was nice to meet you.

    ,

JODI   Yes.
You too.

RITA   Good luck.

    ,

JODI   Right.

TOM kisses JODI on the top of her head.

TOM   You're out of the house.

JODI   I came to find you.

TOM   I didn't go far.

JODI   Can you please take him?

> *JODI passes the child to TOM and leaves.*

> ,

> *TOM turns back and he and RITA look at each other.*

> ,

> *TOM leaves.*

> *RITA watches him go, then looks at her daughter's grave.*

> *It begins to snow.*

> *RITA wraps her jacket around her, and looks up.*

> *The sound of children playing increases as the lights fade.*